Doxie and Roxie go Geocaching

By Brenda Ann Shirey

This book is dedicated to my husband, my children, and of course, to our two dachshunds, Doxie and Roxie

Half the fun of getting there, is the discoveries you make along the way

"Hey Roxie! Wake Up! We are going GEOCACHING!" Doxie said excitedly. "Oh boy! I love geocaching. It is so much fun!" exclaimed Roxie

"Let's ask Avery the cat if she wants to go geocaching too", said Roxie

"Avery, do you want to go with us geocaching?" Doxie asked.

"What is geocaching?" asked Avery

Geocaching is where you use a GPSr (Global Positioning System Receiver), to find hidden containers. All the containers have a log to sign. Some are big and have fun things inside to trade. Others are very small.

They are hidden in the woods and in the city. Sometimes, geocaches are very easy to find and sometimes they are very hard to find. When you are the first to find a geocache, you call it a FTF or "first to find".

When you can't find a geocache, you call it a DNF or "did not find". Sometimes they are missing and the cache owner has to fix them. When you find one, it is a lot of fun.

"Do you want to go with us?" Doxie asked

"No", said Avery. "I don't like that kind of stuff. I will stay home in my sun spot". she purred

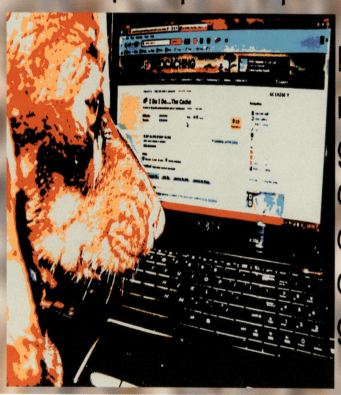

Doxie and Roxie got ready to go geocaching. Roxie checked on the computer to see which caches they wanted to get that day.

Doxie got their GPSr, some extra batteries, lunch, water, and other important stuff for a day of adventure. "We have everything we need", said Doxie. "Let's Go!" Roxie shouted.

"We are getting really close to the cache, Doxie!" called out Roxie. The compass on the GPSr says we are 100 feet away. Start looking around real good. The hint says 'stump'," Roxie said. "Look! Here it is!" called out Doxie, pushing leaves aside. It was hidden in a little hole next to this old rotten stump!"

"This is a big one. It will have fun stuff inside to look at. I hope there is something in there I will want to trade for", Roxie said. They found the log book and signed it with their paw

"What is this?" asked Roxie, pointing at a small trinket hanging on a chain with a metal tag on it. "That is a travelbug, Roxie!" Geocacher's find them and log the number online and then move it into another cache for another cacher to find. See that number?", Doxie said. "That is how you keep track of it"

After carefully putting the geocache back where they found it, so the next person would have as much fun, they headed off to the next cache. When they got home at the end of the day, they told Avery the Cat all about their adventure while they logged their finds online.

Afterwards, they took a nap, because they were dog tired! While they were sleeping, they had dreams about all the exciting things they saw!

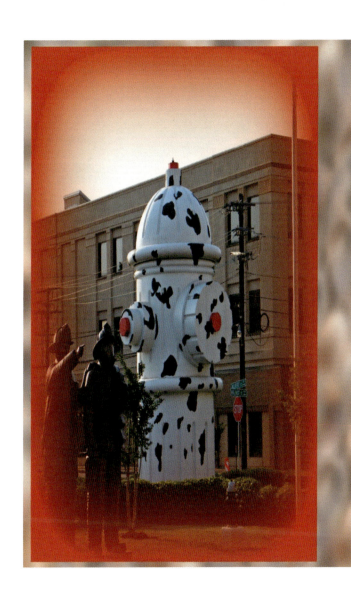

They saw a giant fire hydrant! This one was painted like a Dalmatian dog, the kind that ride with firemen!

They saw a bayou, where all kinds of wildlife live, including many birds and alligators!

This is one of the alligators they saw in the bayou! He has very sharp teeth and claws!

MORE CACHERS PLEASE. THE LAST ONES WERE DELICIOUS!

Up high in a tree, they saw an owl watching over the woods.

Huge Live Oak trees were everywhere. Dogs love trees. These type of trees live 200 - 300 years and provide nice shade during the summer in the south. They are usually covered in moss.

They saw a very scary snake swimming in the water!! Dogs do not like snakes!

This is a crawfish and his home. Crawfish are used as food and bait. Some people even have crawfish as pets! Doxie and Roxie think dogs make better pets. Besides, crawfish can't go geocaching!

Doxie and Roxie can't wait to go geocaching again!

Geocaching is fun for the whole family

If you want to learn more about geocaching, go to www.geocaching.com. It is free to join. Everyone has a nickname they use for geocaching. Our owners nicknames are Sequoia_2, Cajancacheman, and Lil' Tumbleweed.

When you go geocaching, you will see things in your own hometown that you didn't even know were there; including parks, historical sites, and important buildings!

There are also geocaching events all over the world, where geocachers get together to trade stories and help new cachers learn how to cache. Check for an event near you.

~Doxie and Roxie   follow us to the cache...

Made in the USA
Charleston, SC
12 September 2013